I0470235

Andrei Filippov

Shoot-It-Yourself Wedding Video Guide

Thanks to my daughter-in-law Marlowe for editorial help, and to all the wedding parties I have had a pleasure to work with for letting me polish my skills.

This Guide summarizes my experience in covering weddings on two continents in two millenniums, and addressed to video enthusiasts and professionals new to the wedding business. Although it is full of good advices, I am not responsible for the process and the final result of your wedding day coverage. Enjoy reading it, and the rest is up to you. Good luck!

Table of Contents

Glossary

of some terms used in the Guide,
although you probably know most of it anyway

Action shot: indicates the movement in the video, could be the objects' movement, camera movement, or both; often used in reference to "good TV" as opposed to static shoot, sometimes considered as a "boring TV".

Beauty shot: the portion of the video focused on an attractive object, often a close-up.

Jump cut: relates to the video editing process and indicates deliberate or erroneous use of similarly framed shots one after another causing impression of the unsmooth video.

Frame: relates to the outer line of what you see in your viewfinder, might as well be imperative to "compose your shot".

Low angle: relates to the shooting direction. In many cases the camera person would naturally hold the camera at his or her face level. If he/she points the camera up, that would be a low angle shot. Sometimes though the camera person would deliberately hold the camera low and tilt it up to dramatize the shot or to show something unseen from other angle, or to entertain the viewer.

Roll: or "roll and record", same as shoot, or film, industry slang.

Side shot and reverse shot: both indicate position of the camera in relation to the object of interest, aside or behind the object correspondingly.

Wide shot, medium shot or a close-up shot: all relate in general to how much of the object of interest you are going to show. Often replaced in industry jargon by "loose shot", "tight shot", "waist-up", "head-and-shoulders" and many more.

Wedding Day Events to Be Covered

The Wedding Day usually falls into 5 events:

- groom's house;
- bride's house;
- ceremony;
- photo session (or park portion);
- reception.

Depending on how much you want to cover, your ability to travel or to be in two places at the same time and other factors, you may omit groom's house and photo session.

The Ceremony, of course, is the most important part of the day. Coverage of bride and bridesmaids getting ready and the guests at the reception will add some nice details to the final video.

At the final editing stage you may add:

- a photo montage (could be called a slide show, or a "love story") made of the still photos of the couple;
- pre-filmed interviews;
- the rehearsal video;
- and the honeymoon video or slide show.

To summarize, you will choose from the following options:

- Essential: ceremony only.

- Modest: bride's house, ceremony and reception.

- Full day coverage: groom's house, bride's house, ceremony, park portion and reception.

- Luxury package: full day coverage, plus slide show, pre-filmed interview, rehearsal video and honeymoon coverage.

Key Moments to Film at the Groom's House

The idea of the groom's house coverage is to film the guys and the family getting ready for the ceremony. It's fun, it's touching and it is serious, all in one.

The moments here not to be missed:

- the groom and his mother;
- groomsmen having a drink;
- a few words from the groomsmen;
- best wishes from mom and dad;
- outdoor activity;
- house decoration.

The Groom and His Mother

The idea of the shot is simple. The mother is helping her son to start his new family. For the last time she is seeing him as a single man. Show some interaction between the two.

The best and the easiest thing to shoot is mom helping her son with his outfit. Usually the groom is supposed to have a nice corsage attached to his lapel. If the corsage is already in place upon your arrival, you may ask mom to redo it for the camera. If the plan is to do corsages in the church prior to the Ceremony, you may still suggest staging the shot for the camera.

Ask mom to check her son's tie, shirt and jacket. Then comes the corsage. Ask the groom to give his mom a hug and a kiss after she is done with the corsage. Some men would not do that unless being asked.

Shooting the Groomsmen Having a Drink

This should be a cheerful, noisy and casual video. The groom, all the groomsmen, probably mom and dad and close family would form a semicircle around the table. Everybody is cheering and having a drink.

Consult with the groom first if he likes that idea. Actually it makes sense to talk to the bride and the groom beforehand about various aspects of the video coverage and to discuss some key moments of the wedding day.

If both the dad and the best man are going to be present in the shot, split their roles. For example ask dad to pour drinks and the best man to toast, or vice versa. Ask the groom to take his place in the center. Some guys are unbelievably shy, so you may have to ask. The best man stays next to the groom. Make sure you can see everybody. You might as well ask the participants to be able to see you. If they can see you, there is a good chance you'll get them all on tape.

If your lens is not wide enough to include all the groomsmen in the shot, start on the toasting person and the groom. After the toast is said, slowly pan sideways; stay at the end of the line for some time and slowly pan the other way along the line.

Shooting Few Words from the Groomsmen

Practically, it is easier to accomplish when all the groomsmen got together, all dressed up and available for a shoot. This may be a moment just before the photographer starts taking formal shots of the guys with the groom, or, even better, right after. You may film them one by one, but in order to reduce your chance to omit somebody, better take them all at once.

If your camera microphone is good enough, go for it. However, it is preferable to move into a quiet area. You can do this by excusing yourself with the groomsmen to the next quiet room or attracting everybody's attention to the fact of doing impromptu interview. You may do it outside as well, on the backyard or in the front, as long as it is quiet out there. Watch for laundry lines on the background.

Ask the guys to line up, tell them what you are going to do and ask them to keep it short and nice. As soon as the person on either side is ready, start filming one person at a time.

Frame it at head and shoulders, elbows or waist up. After one person has finished, pan slowly to the next one and record the next clip. Carry on until you have got everyone covered.

Thank the groomsmen for the great opportunity. Move along to your next shoot.

Best Wishes from Mom and Dad

This part is similar to Shooting Few Words from the Groomsmen. What makes the difference is while the guys are there to have fun, the parents are usually very busy and may not have much time for you.

So your strategy could be ambushing the parents while they are posing for the formal photos with their son. Approach them as soon as they are done. Find a cozy and quiet spot. If you are in the parents' house, see if you can do it outside, in the front. If you prefer doing it inside, check if there is a wedding photo of mom and dad hung somewhere, probably a black-and-white one. Use it as a background.

Give mom and dad some time to put their thoughts together, then frame and shoot.

Filming Outdoor Activity at the Groom's House

It's assumed that the guys are usually more outgoing, involved in sports, etc. If this is the case, try to set something of that kind outside: throwing football, riding a bike or playing street hockey with the golf clubs. If nothing from sport related activities is acceptable, just nice walk in the neighborhood will do.

For a walking shot, line the guys up on a safe road near the house as you have done so for a Few Words From Groomsmen. Ask the groom to stay in the center, and everybody else on either left or right side. Position yourself, let them walk, and shoot.

Another idea could be the groom and the groomsmen leaving for the church. It might be a fake shot as well as a real one. Depending on the situation it may be a fun video, a romantic stuff or dry documentary style coverage.

How to Shoot Household Decorations

People generally decorate their houses for a wedding day. At the very least they would clean their house up. Some people may buy balloons. Watch for the flowers as well. It is nice to decorate your video with those accents created specifically for the wedding day.

The house may be decorated from outside: check the entrance, the patio, or flower beds.

I once had to shoot a big heart made of the rose petals carefully laid down on the front lawn. It was pointed out in my contract and I was reminded to shoot that heart as soon as I walked in, though only a blind person could have missed it. The shot of the petal heart turned out to be a good opening for that segment of the Wedding Video.

Check as well for some small decorative details in the house: it may be the wedding photos of other family members (mom and dad? older sister?) or a casual photo of a marrying couple stuck on the fridge. It may be an old clock, especially if it shows right time. You don't need to spot and film all these elements at once. It may look even better if you spread them through your video creating a rhythm.

Shooting at Bride's Place

These are key shots you do not want to miss:

- a wedding dress;
- bride getting dressed;
- father meeting the bride;
- bride meeting a flower girl;
- blessing or parents wishes;
- bridesmaids wishes;
- formal photos;
- house decoration;
- bride leaving for the church.

Shooting Wedding Dress

If you get to the bride's place before she has started putting her dress on, you will have a chance to get a shot of just a dress without a bride. The dress will probably be hung on the closet door.

Make sure the white balance is right. Take a wide shot to present The Dress. Come closer; take a slow pan from the tail all the way up to the top. Do some close ups of the details. Bride will put on this dress just once in her life, so make sure to document it meticulously.

Once I was shooting the bride and the

bridesmaids getting ready in a beauty salon, not at home. The bride was stuck in the hairdresser's chair, and the dress was kept in the back room. The back room did not look good enough for my video. I asked the maid of honour to bring the dress to the bride so she could have another look at it. We staged the "approval" sequence right at the hairdresser's chair where it looked much better.

Shooting the Bride Getting Dressed

Ask the bride to call you in the room when she is almost ready. All you need is the last touches. The bride in her beautiful dress, mom and the bridesmaids trying to help. Get a shot of the mom putting earrings or a necklace on the bride, bridesmaids tightening the laces or zipping up the dress.

This may be logically appropriate moment to ask the bride how she is feeling about the ceremony. The brides often feel upbeat or get emotional after having been dressed and ready to be seen by the guests.

Depending on how the bride is feeling, you may suggest videotaping her putting on the garter or the wedding shoes.

Keep it family rated.

Father Meeting the Bride

This is the shot of the father seeing his daughter dressed up as a bride for the first time. After the bride is ready to come to the guests, go ahead and have the dad in position ready to see his daughter. You really need good planning here. Too often there is not enough space for all the participants of the moment. Find the spot for the dad; politely explain where you want him to stay. If bride's room is upstairs, place the dad downstairs, leave some room for the bride after she has come down.

This is going to be a spectacular shot of the bride slowly walking down the stairs. Keep it wide. Follow her almost all the way down, then pan to the dad and capture his reaction. There may be tears, excitement, a short statement, or a hug and a kiss. Whatever it is, that's the shot.

One of my brides simply walked by the dad without paying attention to him, so his reaction was a jaw dropped and panic. The shot was ruined, but I learned the lesson. Now I am asking the brides to make a stop by their dad for it makes good video.

Shooting a Blessing

The blessing is a very popular feature at the French weddings. If the wedding you are working on is not a French one, never mind.

Film the parents' wishes. Parents' wishes at the bride's house are similar to ones at groom's house.

For a blessing you need to set up a still shot as if it was a still photograph. Possible scenario: put the dad on your left, the bride or the groom on your right, kneeled down in front of the dad. Place mom in the center of the frame, but behind the bride or the groom, in the background. Mom is important, but the bride and her dad are the major players in this scene. Now let the dad bless his daughter or son.

This may be emotional scene. If you see emotions on anyone's face, zoom in.

This is a good general rule: Emotions - Zoom In.

The Bride Meeting the Flower Girl

The flower girl is another important participant of the wedding day. She is a shadow of the bride, a little angel, marching ahead of the bride down the aisle, scared by all these strangers surrounding her all day long. She is a future bride and a reflection of the bride in her childhood. Is she not?

This shot is hard to plan. The flower girl may come to bride's house with her parents, usually bride's or groom's friends or family members. The little girl, excited by being dressed up, sees the beautiful bride. The bride is looking at the flower girl.

I wish you luck in getting that shot unstaged. It's quite hard to stage a shot with a little child. If the flower girl does not feel comfortable to be on camera, just leave her alone, and stay away for some time. Get your shot later on.

You might as well try to catch some interaction between the bride and the flower girl while a formal photo is taken. Stay at the distance and shoot with long focus.

Shooting the Bridesmaids' Wishes

Shooting the bridesmaids' wishes is similar to shooting few words from the groomsmen. It is crucial to find the right moment and the right spot.

Ask all the bridesmaids to get together in a quiet room or outside. Choose the background. Girls look good with flowers, so look for a flower bed or a bouquet. Avoid trash bins and laundry lines.

Make sure it does not interfere with the photographer's plan. If the girls are involved in the formal photo session, catch them right after they have finished. Getting them all at once is easier than chasing them one by one; it saves time and assures that they don't repeat themselves.

Line the girls up in a half circle or a straight line. While doing that, try to explain what you are looking for. It should not be a long speech, but rather a short statement or a wish. On average 50% of the bridesmaids would have no idea of what they want to say. Give them suggestions or ask a question. It may be: "congratulations and best wishes on your wedding day", "welcome to the family", or simply "I love you". Start on either side with one of the bridesmaids who is feeling the most confident. Film one person at a time without or with stopping your camera, depending on the situation.

If you feel that the girls are excited and up to doing something crazy (singing a funny song, dancing a cancan, playing grass hockey with golf clubs, etc), suggest to stage a shot.

Filming during the Formal Bridal Photo Shoot

It is exciting to see the photographer working on the portraits, especially if you are familiar with his or her approach.

What it gives you in practical sense is some action. The difference between your camera and a still camera is that you can shoot the girls approaching and leaving the spot. They look different: some may be shy, others could feel more comfortable being on the spot. Their looks, their smiles, put it all on video. Use a variety of shots. Alternate wide shot of the entire scene with extreme close up of the bride or the flower girl. Or start on the close up of a bouquet and zoom out to the group shot.

Do groups in action, people setting for a shot. Use close ups to capture the reaction of people interacting with each other.

Should I Film the Bride Leaving for the Church?

It is up to you and the bride. The general rule is that you should be in the Church ahead of time. If you are the only cameraman covering entire wedding day, I strongly recommend you not to film that for real. You want to leave bride's house at least 30 minutes before she does. Offer to do a fake shot instead.

As for the shot itself, do it in a sequence. This will take some patience on both sides, yours and the bridal party's. You want the shot of the bride leaving the house, so shoot the house first. Ask the bridal party to line up behind the front door: bride goes first, mom and dad to follow, and then come the bridesmaids. Position yourself outside on the side (you'll see why) of the driveway. You should be able to get full body shot of each person coming out of the door.

There may be variations of that shot. For example, you may limit the participants to the bride and her parents. Or you can add the made of honour. It's always handy to have her around. The family may suggest de-ribboning ceremony, at which the mom would cut the ribbon at the door to let the bride out.

When you are ready to shoot, ask the bridal party to start coming out and to proceed towards the limo. Keep rolling and let the bride walk by you (that's why you want to stay aside). Run ahead, and take a position by the limo in front of the back door - you want to see bride's face when she approaches the limo and gets in the car. Don't let her completely in, those wedding dresses are not very comfortable for getting in and out of the car. Pan off to the limo (bridesmaids, house, clouds, etc.), thank the bride and drive to the church.

Key Moments to Shoot at the Christian Non-Orthodox Wedding Ceremony

Here is your list:

- church exterior;
- arrival of the guests;
- arrival of the bride;
- bridesmaids walking down the aisle;
- the bride and her father walking down the aisle;
- the groom meeting the bride;
- candle shot (optional);
- readings (optional);
- exchange of vows;
- exchange of the rings;
- signing ceremony;
- communion;
- announcement of the marriage;
- married couple leaving the church;
- group photo on the front steps;
- guests greetings;
- bride and groom leaving the spot.

Shooting Church Exterior

The exterior of the church may be an integral part of the wedding day coverage. It is not a priority shot, but rather a good locator shot and a meaningful transition between parts of your video.

Do this shot after you have finished setting up inside and right before you go get your next shot, the arrival of the bride.

Walk away from the front entrance far enough to get entire building in the frame. Try a low angle shot; it often gives buildings a majestic look. Wait until there is no traffic and roll on it for 5 or 6 seconds.

Arrival of the Guests

The arrival of the guests to the ceremony is not an essential part of the wedding video unless the couple insists on a very detailed coverage. Arrival shots will slow the video unless you keep them short and vivid.

You may get few shots of the most important people, like grandparents or members of the bridal party. Don't forget, you have to be well prepared to work inside the church during the ceremony. Filming the guests may take away some time needed for setting inside, so be careful. And in any case keep it short.

Another option is to videotape some guests who arrived earlier inside the church. You may probably film the groom, groom's family and groomsmen being busy taking guests to their sits and doing their last minute preparations.

But don't miss arrival of the bride. Keep in mind: she is the most important character in your video.

Arrival of the Bride

The most typical form of arrival is pulling over in a limousine or some fancy car, or the horse carriage to the front entrance of the church. Make sure in advance that this is the case. Variations might be as follows: arrival in a horse-drawn carriage (in a balloon, on foot, by bus) to the side (back) door, on the parking lot or to stop by the gate 300 feet away from the entrance, you name it.

First, get a shot of the vehicle slowing down and pulling over to where it is supposed to stop. You may lower the camera and shoot at low angle, or stay on the top of the front steps and shoot from above. After the car (or horse, etc.) has stopped, get closer, and position yourself by the door, where the bride is supposed to appear. Let the photographer to take photos with the bride, her dad and a limo. You might film that as well.

The next moment is very important. Place yourself strategically where you would be able to get a clear shot of the bride and her dad starting and finishing their walk all the way from the limo to the church entrance.

Don't compete with the photographer, make friends instead. If the photographer takes one side of the door, take another one. You don't want him or her to stick between you and the bride.

Follow the bride and the dad to the entrance. If they slow down before entering the church, slowly pan off to the top of the building to complete the shot. Make sure it looks great and proceed inside. The clock is ticking.

Shooting the Bridesmaids Walking Down the Aisle

This is one of the key shots in the ceremony and you don't want to miss it. Sometimes the timeframe of the ceremony is too tight and the bridesmaids do their walk down the aisle at the same time the bride is arriving to the front entrance. If you are using one camera, you may miss that shot. Talk to the couple and check what the plan is.

Position yourself at the front end of the aisle next to the groom in a way that allows the bridesmaids to take their spots in front of the altar. You may have to position yourself on a balcony above the altar. It will depend on the rules set by the church or the priest performing the ceremony.

Don't miss the flower girl and the ring boy. If they are part of the ceremony, they will be there, in the head of the procession, or at the very end just before the bride. If you are shooting from the top of the altar, and you are positioned aside from the center, you may not be able to see the children. They will be blocked by standing guests. But you could still get a shot of them appearing in front of the altar. If you see them clearly, frame and roll, slowly zooming out in order to keep the frame. Follow your camera until the kids have taken their spots.

If you have managed to get a shot of the flower girl and the ring boy, filming the bridesmaids is a piece of cake. Frame on the first girl, roll and follow the camera until she is on the front. Stop camera, frame it on the next girl, roll and follow, and so on. If the aisle is too long, start filming from the moment the first girl is half way through the aisle. Otherwise the first shot may be unproportionally long.

The girls may follow each other very closely. In this case you should roll on the first girl while letting the next girl walk into the shot. Do the same with each bridesmaid. When the last girl is in your shot, follow her until she stops in front of the altar and you have all the bridesmaids in your shot. Stop there, get ready for appearance of the bride.

Filming the Bride Walking Down the Aisle

The appearance of the bride is another key moment of the wedding day coverage. As soon as you are done with shooting the bridesmaids walking down the aisle and taking their spots, prepare yourself for the appearance of the bride. You won't have much time. If you are allowed to move, position yourself in front of the altar, besides and slightly behind the groom in such a way that you have access to every moment of the following sequence without stopping to roll.

Frame on the bride and the father and roll continuously while zooming out slowly. Possible obstacles are: the photographer walking backwards in front of the bride and taking pictures, and the guests stepping in the aisle in front of you, trying to compete with the photographer. You should talk to the photographer ahead of time and let him or her know where you are going to stay and ask for cooperation. The guests are different story, you can't ban them from blocking the bride, but they are a natural part of the ceremony, so don't worry too much about the guests in your shot.

You may want to show groom's reaction. For that purpose you could zoom out and pan off the bride and show groom's profile or ¾ reverse shot, depending on your position. One thing I know for sure is that many brides want to have this shot in the video, so try your best.

Pan back to the bride, she must be closer at that moment. Or you might stop your camera instead right after the groom's reaction shot, reframe and refocus on the bride and start rolling again. At some point the bride and her father will stop and let the groom approach them. The dad would take the veil off his daughter's face and pass her on to the groom. You may want to follow the groom and come a little closer. Stay on all three, and after they are done with all the kisses and handshakes, move carefully backwards to let the bride and the groom to proceed to the altar to meet the priest.

Keep rolling continuously and move backwards very carefully. You don't want to hurt anybody in the bridal party or the ceremony officiant.

Shooting a Candle Lighting

Candle lighting is getting more and more popular at wedding ceremonies, and the married couples want to see that captured on tape.

For this part of the wedding ceremony three candles, two smaller ones and a big one in between are placed on the altar. The mothers of both the bride and the groom approach the altar, each receiving already lit candles from the priest. They light small candles sitting on the table and leave the big one unlit. Wait until the end of the marriage ceremony, we'll get to it.

If you are allowed to move around, position yourself behind the candles, so you can see moms' faces. If not, still try to include as much as possible in your shot. After staying wide while shooting the action shot, you may want to shoot a close up of the candles.

In some cases the bride and the groom light the side candles. But it won't change much in terms of shooting technique.

Do I Have to Shoot Readings?

Readings are integral part of the ceremony, but I really doubt you want to put them on your final video. Audio is usually poor; you may not be able to come close enough to get a good shot. If you think this may happen, talk the bride out of shooting entire readings. Instead offer to include a shot of the ceremony participants coming up to the podium and setting up for the reading. Then you can insert a transition shot: wide shot of all the guests, close up shots of close family, and, of course, the bride and the groom. After transition shot you may establish the next participant, and so on.

Keep in mind, if you have to shoot the entire reading, you will be limited in getting the reaction shots I have just mentioned.

Videotaping the Exchange of Vows

This portion of your video is the most crucial one. If you don't shoot that, forget about the rest of the day. During that ceremony the bride and the groom would normally stand in front of the altar facing each other. In rare occasions they may be facing the priest, so it is good idea to find out what is going to happen in your particular case. Then they would repeat after the priest or read out loud from their notes or by heart the vows to be a husband and a wife, to be faithful in good time and in bad, and so on.

Your mission as a cameraman is to capture the entire event with clean framing from the best possible angle and with good audio.

For the first part, you don't want to have any objects such as candles or flowers between your camera and the marrying couple. The frame should be clean, period. At this point we are arriving to the second part, which is the best possible angle.

You will not always be able to use the best desirable spot, so try your best exploring the options you have. If the bride and the groom are going to face each other, the best spot for you will be in the central aisle, facing the altar and the couple. Move quickly with your tripod, or handheld, to the aisle and position yourself behind the marrying couple. What you get in the frame will be the bride on your left, the groom on your right and the priest or the minister, facing the camera, in between.

If you are not allowed to move freely during the ceremony, position yourself on the groom's side of the church, so you can see the bride's face. If you have to choose between showing the bride or the groom, always go for the bride. She is just more important.

There is a priest in one particular church who allows shooting the ceremony only from the balcony located right above the altar. He does not let the cameramen move during the entire ceremony. At least that provides the opportunity for better angle to cover the exchange of vows.

It brings us to the audio issue. Since we are unable to see the groom's face, we have to make sure the audio is impeccable. For that purpose you should use wireless microphone. The lapel microphone (sometimes called lav, or bag, or clip-on) is set on the groom's jacket, thus providing audio for both groom's and bride's parts as well as for the priest. The microphone is plugged into a transmitter. Make sure you have brand new reliable battery in the transmitter prior to the ceremony. Don't take chances!

Be in the church at least 30 minutes prior to the ceremony. Find the groom and set up the microphone. Put it on the lapel, preferably on the groom's left side (your right side), close to the bride. Hide the transmitter in his inside pocket. Make an audio test to make sure you can hear sound clearly in the camera. There should not be any irrelevant noises, such as interference, squeaking, cracking, etc. Stress out that the microphone should not be turned off until the end of the ceremony.

As for framing, you can keep the same frame for the entire exchange of vows or you may zoom in on the groom's face, then pan over to the bride's face, or vice versa, and then zoom out. Don't use too much movement. More important is to capture entire dialog, the interaction from beginning to end. Be careful, it is a once in a lifetime event. They are not going to do it again just for the camera. But good planning, giving yourself time for preparation, reliable equipment, fresh batteries and quick thinking will be your best friends.

Shooting the Exchanging of the Rings

The exchanging of the rings follows the exchanging of the vows. You can naturally continue filming the ceremony. You might as well change the framing and go a bit wider or tighter.

Usually the priest or the minister would ask the best man to pass him the rings for the blessing, or he would take the rings from the plate. That moment may be quite awkward to shoot with one camera. You don't want to leave your spot even for a moment, so probably just omit the blessing, stop rolling and use this time to adjust your focus on bride's or groom's hand.

If you have finished shooting vows on the wide shot, you may start the exchange of the rings with a close up of the groom's hand placing the ring on the bride's hand. Than start gently zooming out and show the faces and the hands in one frame. You want to see the groom and the bride saying their parts of that ceremony as well.

After the groom's part is over you can zoom in on bride's hand placing the ring on the groom's hand. Then zoom out again.

When the exchanging of rings is over, stay wide and let the priest or the minister proclaim the couple a husband and a wife. At this point you may start slowly zooming in on the man kissing his wife for the first time.

Shooting a Communion

Communion is a traditional part of the Catholic Wedding Ceremony.

Position yourself in front of the Altar. The first key moment is when the bride and the groom are taking Communion: zoom in on the couple having bread and wine.

The next key moment is when the bride and the groom are giving Communion to their guests.

You don't need to shoot the whole ceremony. Covering the bridal party and the close family taking Communion will probably be enough.

Use the rest of the time to get some more side and reverse shots.

Shooting the Signing Ceremony

The newly married couple proceeds to sign a register right after Communion. Take your spot in front of the signing table, most likely next to the photographer. Make sure there is no bouquet or other obstacles between the camera and the register book.

The bride signs the register first. You may start with a wide shot of the bride signing the book, the groom standing by his bride and the priest or the minister on the opposite side.

It is sufficient to videotape one signature for each person.

To avoid a jump cut, use transitions. For example: film all three while the bride signs the book as the opening shot of the segment, stop rolling after the bride completes first signature. Frame on the groom's face and start rolling when he starts taking a seat to sign a register. Let him put his first signature, then stop your camera, zoom out wide to see the bride, the groom, the priest, the best man and the maid of honor, all five people around the table. Start rolling after the best man goes to the table to sign the register, and so on.

Filming the Newlyweds Leaving the Church

First of all, take a spot in the central aisle facing the altar. You will be going backwards, so make your intentions clear to the photographer. It will be better for you to stay on the right hand side of the photographer. In this case you will be able to see the photographer on your left and to coordinate your movements along with his or hers.

The segment starts with the announcement and congratulations from the priest. Frame on all three: the priest and the newly married couple. You may want to start rolling a bit earlier, especially if you are planning to edit the video. Keep it on the three through entire announcement. Hold it like that while the guests are giving the couple their applause.

After few seconds of applause the Wedding March begins to play giving you a signal to start slowly backing up toward the exit. If the couple does not follow you, slow down, keep rolling and beckon them to follow you. Keep it wide all the time and control framing by adjusting the distance between you and the couple.

Keep going backwards to the end of the aisle, or almost to the end, and then make a side step to your right or left into the empty row or behind the back row. You may want to check

your options in advance. Hold the same angle,
let the couple leave the frame and keep on
rolling on the bridal party and the close family
following the married couple. You can pan up
on the altar in order to make a transition to
your next shot.

Videotaping During a Group Photo Shoot after the Wedding Ceremony

Usually, if the weather permits, the newly
married couple has their photo taken with all
the guests. Depending on the photographer it
may be a small festival on its own, or a well
organized event. For the first case see Guests
Greetings, for the second, coordinate with the
photographer.

While the photographer is putting the guests in
place, shoot the action: smiling faces,
handshakes, babies, interacting family
members, etc. You can walk along the front row
with your camera rolling after everyone is in
place. Approach the couple and ask them about
their feelings after the ceremony.

It may as well be good time to take the wireless
microphone away.

Step back so you can see all the guests in your
wide shot, zoom in on the couple. When more
or less everybody is paying attention to the
photographer, start rolling and slowly zoom out
to complete the segment on a wide shot.

You may need to adjust your plan if there is something special like releasing doves, tossing rose petals, blowing bubbles, etc., taking place. It's good to be informed about such an event in advance.

Guests Greetings

Along with taking a big group photo on the front steps of the church or the hall, or other place that accommodated the wedding ceremony, there is a lot of interaction happening right before, after and during the taking of the photo. And that is exactly what you want to capture - the interaction.

It may be the best man shaking groom's hand, grandmother giving the bride a kiss, parents on both sides greeting each other in their new status. You won't be able to catch everything, the couple will be very likely drawn apart by the guests, and that's OK since you don't need to shoot everything anyway.

Key moments to look for:

- the newlyweds looking at their brand new rings after leaving the church;
- bridal party members greeting the newly married couple;
- the parents on both sides (very important);
- close family with the babies;

- the grandparents.

You may choose to shoot it wide, coming close to the action, shooting from your raised hands when necessary. You may shoot it tight (zoomed in) from the steps down. Or mix a bit of everything. Start from establishing the scene: show the couple's faces first. Then you may shoot from behind, paying more attention to the guests' faces. Combine wide shots with close ones.

Shooting the Newlyweds Leaving after the Wedding Ceremony

After everybody is done greeting the newly married couple and wishing them well, and after the group photo is taken, the couple will leave for the photo shoot, for the reception, for the honeymoon, or just to take some rest.

This moment is important as a closure for the ceremony segment of your video. If the couple is leaving in a limo, the chauffeur may offer them Champagne. Shoot the bottle, the cork being crack open, wine being poured into the glasses, new husband and wife cheering up and giving each other a kiss. You may need to direct them as well.

Get a shot of the couple getting into the car. Position yourself in such a way that you can see their faces rather than their backs. You might as well ask the driver to roll down the window for that shot. Get the shot of the happy couple and their friends inside the limo. Most people don't ride limos very often, so it will be appropriate to show the significance of the moment.

Let the driver know that you are going to get a shot of the limo leaving the spot. If the limo has the "Just married" sign on the rear, you may start on the close up of that sign. Start zooming out after the car starts moving away.

You may as well start with the front of the car at a low angle. Let the limo drive by, revealing the church and the crowd waving good bye to the couple.

Christian Orthodox Wedding Ceremony

Christian Orthodox wedding ceremony is quite different from the Non-Orthodox Ceremony. First of all, it may be Greek, Russian, Ukrainian or Lebanese. They all have very much in common with some differences as well.

Prior to filming in the church, find out whether you are allowed in front of the altar where you could see bride's and groom's faces, or if you have to stay behind the marrying couple. There are usually some restrictions different from church to church and from one priest to another, so be prepared. Discuss the range of your movement with the priest.

The altar itself in the Orthodox Church is a sanctuary decorated with icons and lights with an ornamented door in the center. Nobody but the priest is allowed inside. You may be allowed to position yourself just outside that door on the groom's or the bride's side, so you could see both the priest and the couple.

The couple does not speak much during the ceremony. In the Russian Church the priest usually asks if the bride and the groom have been baptized as Orthodox Christians, and after they confirm that, the questioning goes on. In the rest of Orthodox Churches that first question may be skipped and the priest proceeds to the next part, asking if the bride and the groom have come on their own will and if they have not been committed (or promised) to someone else. This questioning may happen at the door, as soon the couple enters the church or in front of the altar prior to the ceremony. After the priest is satisfied with the answers, the ceremony commences, and the couple stays silent until it's over.

You need to shoot the priest blessing the rings and placing them on bride's and groom's fourth finger of the right hand. It may as well be the best man who places the rings on groom's and bride's hands, or they may help each other. The ring usually goes half way through and stays like that until the end of the ceremony.

Another key moment is crowning. The priest blesses two crowns, asks the bride and the groom to kiss the crowns and passes the crowns on to the best man or to the best man and the maid of honour (witnesses, friends, "druzhki" might be the other names of those participants). The crowns are being held above marrying couple's heads and then later may be placed on their heads as the ceremony goes along. Then the couple is offered red wine similar to Catholic tradition. The priest holds the cup in his hands and lets the couple to finish the wine.

The culmination of the crowning is a processional walk around the altar table. The priest leads the procession followed by the bride and the groom and then by the best man and the maid of honour. The ceremony includes three circles around the table and is considered to be a wedding culmination, so keep rolling on all three rounds.

At the end the priest, while standing in the altar door, invites the couple to come closer and talks to them in plain language wishing them well and welcoming them to keep coming to the church.

During the ceremony the priest would be going into the altar and back outside, reading from the bible and singing. You should ask the couple prior to the ceremony if they want you to shoot everything he says. If they do, just continue rolling all the time, especially if you don't understand the language. If the couple lets you use your own discretion, do some beauty shots between shooting key moments: candles, icons, parents, children in the audience, reaction shots from the bridal party, wide shot from the back of the church, etc.

After the ceremony is over, the couple leaves the church in pretty much the same way as they would be leaving the Catholic Church.

Filming at the Photo Session after the Wedding Ceremony

In many cases the newlywed couple and the bridal party will go for more formal photos. That is the moment when both families and the bridal party can pose for pictures.

Since you are going to follow the party, talk to the photographer to find out the location of the photo shoot. It is usually the photographer's call, or at least his input is considered. Make sure to stay informed in case the location is changed at the last moment.

At the location, take a mix of beauty and action shots. The bridal party dressed up, children, interaction within the party, and especially between bride and groom.

You don't have to focus on the formal photos only, but don't forget to shoot some. Take a good balance of both families. If you pay more attention to bride's family, for example, the groom's family may be disappointed, and vice versa.

If you are hired to do the job and get paid by the parents of one side, you don't want to disappoint them.

As it applies to any good video, mix a variety of shots: wide, medium, close, extra wide, extra close, static, movement, etc.

Shooting a Wedding Reception

There are few moments you want to cover:

- cocktail hour;
- decoration of a banquet hall;
- receiving line;
- bridal party introduction;
- Prayer;
- toasts;
- speeches;
- gift table;
- formal dances;
- games;
- cake cutting;
- the guests dancing;
- bouquet toss;
- garter toss;
- sweet table.

Shooting during Cocktail Hour

Cocktail hour usually precedes the wedding dinner and starts about an hour prior to reception. The main target is the guests. Use your judgment on when to start shooting. You don't want to videotape an empty lobby, but on the other you need some room to walk around. So don't wait until it gets too crowded.

Look around for accents: guest book, engagement photo, fruit salads, chocolate fountain, jazz band, chef making flames while cooking shrimp, open bar, etc. There is nothing unnecessary around: every single accent was thought through by the married couple. Don't miss a thing, and your effort will be appreciated.

While shooting the guest book, don't shoot just the book, but the guests signing the book. While shooting an engagement photo, shoot the guests looking at the photo and their reaction as well. Try to capture action rather than static objects.

As for the guests themselves, you may limit yourself to videotaping the people mingling, buying drinks, picking food (don't show them eating though), greeting parents. Or you may walk around asking people for a short message: a joke, a greeting or a short story. It depends on what the couple wants, as well as how responsive the guests are, so try your best.

Cocktail hour may be the best (or the only) time for you to get ready for filming at the dinner, so use your time wisely. You don't need full hour to get a glimpse of a cocktail party.

Shooting a Banquet Hall Decoration

Marrying people put a big deal of an effort into countless details of a wedding day celebration. One thing everybody forgets after being as far as half way through a wedding reception is how nicely decorated the hall is.

It's your duty to keep that beauty captured for eternity.

During cocktail hour or prior to it enter the big room and get few shots. You don't need much, but make sure you have a wide shot or a pan through the room, shot of a head table, a single dinner table decorated with the centerpiece. Look around and as you see the accomplishment of a human effort, get it covered.

If you are lucky, get a shot of a waiter lighting candles. If it is too dark for your camera, ask the caterer to bring the dimmers up.

Shooting Receiving Line

Receiving line signals the end of the cocktail party and invitation to the wedding dinner. For that purpose the newly married couple, parents on both sides and the bridal party are lining up by the main entrance into the hall. The guests line up in order to be met and greeted by the party and to proceed to their tables.

For the wedding of an average size of a couple hundred guests this procedure may take between 20 and 40 minutes. Of course you do not need to roll on during all that time. Make sure to get the most important guests on tape, such as grandparents and close family, guests from overseas, nice looking guests and guests with babies. If there are some gifts to be given out, film some of the gifts as well.

In terms of approaching the line, get an inventory:

- a wide shot to establish the line;
- a medium shot while moving along the line, focus on the bridal party faces;
- a reverse: shoot from behind the bridal party, this time shoot the guests faces; start wide and pan from side to side, than go closer to show their reaction;
- close ups of each person in the bridal party from both angles; show smiles, amusement, and the happiness of the moment.

You should get enough footage during first five minutes. Then enjoy cocktails and appetizers.

Bridal Party Introduction

The couple may skip the receiving line, but the bridal party introduction is important ceremonial part and ought to be videotaped properly. Success depends on logistics similar to shooting the bride and the bridesmaids walking down the aisle in the church.

Find out what entrance is going to be used. There may be two different entrances: one for the couple and another one for the rest of the bridal party. Position yourself considering the following:

- you should be able to get a well lit walking shot from point A to point B. Point A is the door, and point B is the head table or the dance floor. You will definitely need your camera light. Use extra lights if necessary;

- you should be able to get a shot clear of the guests or caterers lurking in front of you. With all respect to the guests and especially to the people working hard to make the wedding happen, at this point focus on the bridal party;

- you should be able to get a clear shot of the bride and groom after all the guests stand up for their entrance.

Considering all of the above you may position yourself:

- at the door;

- half way between the door and the head table;

- or by the head table.

Each position bears its benefits and disadvantages. See what works better for you.

The introduction ceremony is usually an impromptu event, and does not go smoothly all the time. Prepare yourself to continuous rolling. Your queue would most likely be the DJ's or MC's line: "without further ado I would like to introduce...". Press REC and take your thumb away from that red button no matter what. Keep rolling and fix problems later during editing.

Talk to MC or DJ (depending on who is going to announce the entering party) before the introduction to find out the order of appearance, the path the party is going to take and if there is anything you may not expect.

For the entrance of the newly married couple shoot some reaction from the guests as well: happy faces, cheering and clapping.

Sometimes the bride and the groom make their first dance a part of the introduction ceremony. If that's the plan, make sure you have enough batteries and tapes.

Shooting a Prayer at the Reception

Prayer precedes the wedding dinner. Either a priest or the family elder would come to the microphone to read the Prayer.

You have two options to position yourself:

- shooting from the position set up for the speeches;
- or shooting handheld from aside of the

podium.

Either way you should have your audio set up in advance, normally it should be done during cocktail hour or prior to it.

Keep it medium, waist up. You may zoom out and pan on the head table after the Prayer is over.

Shooting Speeches at the Wedding Reception

Speeches may be held after the dinner or throughout the dinner between the courses. The speakers may use podium and house microphone, or they may stand up at their tables and speak into the DJ's wireless mic. You should be ready to either situation.

If the speeches are going to be held at the podium, find the best position for your tripod and a light. In your circumstances it will be determined by:

- close enough to be able to zoom in and pan from the speaker to the head table and back, and far enough to leave a clear view of the podium for the guests;

- out of the caterers way: you don't want to make enemies, try to be friends with all your colleagues;

- close enough to the power source of your light.

For safety reasons always cover the cables with Gaffer tape or tunnel tape.

If the speeches are going to be held at the tables, you have no choice but to shoot handheld moving quickly from person to person. Make sure you always have enough tapes and batteries. Some guests may have long speeches, especially after few drinks.

If the speakers are going to use house microphone installed on the podium, you may set up your microphone next to it. The easiest would be to attach lav microphone to the house microphone.

If the speakers are going to use the DJ's wireless microphone, you may:

- try to plug into the DJ's system (at your own risk);
- attach your microphone to the DJ's microphone (looks ugly on tape);
- or set the microphone at the loudspeaker.

For the last option you may want to use a microphone on a stand pointed at the loudspeaker, or hang your lavaliere microphone from above the speaker. The sound from the speaker may be very loud, so adjust transmitter's level low enough to avoid distortion.

As for the speeches themselves, stay on a medium shot, zoom in if the speaker becomes sentimental, pan off to the head table to show bride's and groom's reaction. Pan to other bridal party members within your range during bride's and groom's speech when they mention bridesmaids, groomsmen or parents.

Shooting Gift Table at the Wedding Reception

Wedding guests show up for a reception carrying gifts in either monetary or tangible form. For the former they deliver the envelopes with cash, cheques or gift certificates. For the latter, they carry boxes or gift bags. All the treasures are placed on the gift table for display purposes. Envelopes may be put in a slotted box (piggy-bank) or a fancy bird cage.

All you need is patience. Let all the gifts, or at least most of them get collected. It may happen during receiving line or cocktail hour.

Start shooting at one end of the gift table and keep rolling panning camera slowly towards another end. Use a few close-ups of the most spectacular details. Use you camera light if necessary.

Shooting Formal Dances at the Wedding Reception

There may be few formal dances at the wedding reception:

- bride and groom (this may be the only formal dance at all, but it may be performed twice);
- bride and her father;
- groom and his mother;
- bridal party - groomsmen and bridesmaids (may be called depending on tradition in your area).

Depending on ethnic and religious background of the wedding participants there may as well be hora, sirtaki, khorovod, bride's brother socks dance, etc. Check with the couple or with the MC or DJ for details.

Shoot entire first dance non-stop. Keep rolling camera no matter what. I usually roll on other dances continuously as well. You can always cut them shorter while editing if the customers wish it so.

I strongly recommend using a light to shoot a formal dance. Two lights, a stationary light and a camera light – is even better. Inquire with the DJ or the band if they are planning to use strong fancy lighting for the formal dances. If not, set yours up. It is a common opinion that people do not like bright lights at the reception. They would not like grainy shadows moving on their foggy video either if there is not enough light for your camera.

You may move slowly around the dancing couple or stand still on the floor or on a riser (on a chair, table, etc.). Moving the camera gives some action to the shot. Three minutes of continuous dancing filmed from the same angle may look boring even to your couple. However, it takes some practice or special equipment (or both) to be able to deliver a stable shot while shooting with moving camera.

If you are not equipped with a steadycam or at least a dolly, think of your camera as a jockey on a horse. It may be hard to think of yourself as a horse, but if it helps the final product, give it a try.

Choose the right background especially if you are shooting from a fixed position. You don't want your couple to dance in front of the kitchen, washroom or EXIT sign. Locate yourself in such a way that you can see the head table or the guests in the background. Same if you are planning to move: avoid ugly backgrounds as much as possible. Come closer to the dancing couple if the background is turning flat or looks unpleasant. Back up to get a wider shot to incorporate a dancing couple and larger area of background if it is relevant and looking good.

Keep in mind: it is a formal and sometimes very touching moment of the day (although sometimes it may be not, some people talk business while dancing). Get closer or zoom in when they look at each other or give each other a kiss or bow to the guests at the end of the dance.

Cake Cutting

The newly married couple cutting the cake is a quick but symbolic part of a wedding ceremony.

You can do it:

- prior to the reception if the official photographer decides to do it at that time; ask the couple if they want that portion of the video to be done along with the cake cutting photo;
- after the main course before desert;
- at any other time on couple's call.

If you do it along with the official photographer, let him or her set up the shot and complete the session. After the photo is taken, step in. Let the couple stay the way the photographer set them up and shoot.

If you are on your own, choose a proper background. Avoid flat walls, open kitchen doors, EXIT signs, etc. Preferable backgrounds: flower arrangement, guest tables, head table, anything related to the bright side of the special day. Ask if the couple wants the cutting to be announced by the MC, so the guests willing to take a photo may join the set with their cameras.

Ask the couple what part of the cake they are going to slice, if they are going to try it or to give each other to try and ask them for a kiss after they are done cutting.

Start with medium wide shot of both the bride and the groom in your shot, pan down to the cake being cut, stay on the cake, pan up to the couple for a kiss or on them trying the cake. Stop your camera, thank the couple and let them go back to the party. Shoot a close up of the cut and the details of the cake.

Shooting the Guests Dancing

You may need to shoot one or two dances: one slow, another one fast, unless the couple asks for more. You may shoot a series of segments of various dances to show the party unfolding. Whatever is your idea, check if this is exactly what your couple wants.

From technical point of view, I would not recommend using stationary lights, as it will ruin the party's mood. Rely on the DJ's lights and your camera light. Combine both and stay within the range of the lights' strength.

In order to make the video more exciting, vary your camera angle: shoot from a low angle, then from your hands raised. Watching music videos will give you an idea of shooting technique.

Be careful with the aperture while using your

camera light and moving fast at the same time.
Keep the dancing crowd properly exposed.

Shooting the Bouquet Toss

It is almost the end of your day. Often the DJ
or the band will invite all the single girls onto
the dance floor. Check if you have any
preferences in terms of better lighting of
background. Consider possible obstacles up
high, such as oversized lighting fixture or
decorations hanging across and over the dance
floor. If you think that placing the girls and the
bride your way would be preferable, don't be
shy, get involved and politely point to where
you want them to stay.

Get a shot of the single girls getting together,
pushing and giggling. Then position yourself in
front of the bride, so you can clearly see her
face, the bouquet and the girls in the back. Play
by ear depending on how the event unfolds.
The DJ may count to three, stopping at two and
a half, two and three quarters, and then start
all over again, the bride may fake the toss, etc.
Just keep rolling and watch it. You can move a
bit closer and farther to vary the shot while the
excitement is growing, but keep the camera on
the bride and the bouquet.

When the flowers go flying, follow the bouquet
with your camera and start moving towards the
lucky catcher. Get reactions from the other
girls, somebody has to be upset. Get back to

the lucky one: most likely she will approach the bride or will be approached by the bride.

It is all about celebration and people having a good time. Enjoy it and add some party mood to your video.

Shooting the Garter Toss

This normally happens right after the bouquet toss. As with the bouquet toss, the DJ or the band will call all the single men to the dance floor.

The bride will be seated in the chair in the center of the dance floor. If there is nobody to offer a chair, take the initiative, borrow the chair from the closest table and place it the way you like. Consider lighting and the background.

In most cases the groom is supposed to kneel down, reach under bride's dress and pull the garter from her leg with his teeth or hands. Use low angle technique. Shoot with your hands lowered using wide angle. Show the groom diving underneath the dress, pan up to the bride's face (reaction shot), pan down back to the groom, move over - show reaction of the guests and single men if you have enough time for that. But don't miss the moment when the groom emerges from under the dress with the garter in his teeth.

The rest is similar to the bouquet toss shooting.

This will probably end your day as a wedding cameraman. Next section contains some general noted relevant to entire day rather than to some specific part.

On A General Note

Make Friends with the DJ

The DJ is your working colleague, normally only during reception. Your good working relationship with the entertainment person (or a team, lets call it DJ to make it simple) is important for a number of reasons.

Schedule

Unless the evening schedule is ultimately dictated by Master of Ceremony, the DJ is in control. He may consult the marrying couple during the night, but in most cases he moves his schedule along according to his own understanding of the rhythm and pace of the party. First of all, make sure you are aware of upcoming events. Often the DJ substitutes the MC in part or in full. He usually knows the timeframe of the evening and the kind of activities planned for the evening. Tell him that you are trying to do good work for the bride and the groom and point out the importance of keeping you aware of any changes in the schedule.

Time to go home

If you are a guest or a family member planning to shoot the wedding video, skip this paragraph and go to Audio Issues. If you are working for hire, than you may finish your work significantly earlier or later depending on the DJ. Normally the last thing on your list would be a bouquet and garter toss. It may happen at 10PM or after midnight. Making friends with the DJ may help you to negotiate favorable timing for the last event to be covered.

Audio Issues

Check with the DJ, what is his plan in regards to the toasts and the speeches. If all the speeches are to be delivered from the podium through the house audio system, do your installation without bringing the DJ into equation. But if there is no microphone provided by banquet hall, the DJ will come in handy with his wireless microphone and audio system. In this situation, you will probably need to plug into the DJ's mixer board. It may be a challenge for many DJ's to provide an audio feed, so make friends before the problem has arisen.

Organizing Tapes and Batteries during the Day

Having enough tapes and batteries for the day is crucial. You need a sufficient amount of both.

Take at least 4 hours worth of tapes and 6 hours worth of batteries. Remember to bring a battery charger.

Get the tapes and batteries organized in your camera bag.

Keep tapes in their cases, all properly labeled, before going to the shoot. The easiest thing would be to place clear labels on each tape. You might date them in advance. Have a pen or two handy; make notes on the tape/box before putting it in the bag after using the tape. The fastest way to mark the tapes would be placing consecutive numbers on them. If you have extra time, put down some additional information as well, such as "groom's house," or "reception-1" and so on.

Mark all your batteries with numbers or colours to avoid wasting time figuring out which battery is charged and which one is not. Keep your battery charger plugged into the AC/DC adapter in your car during the travel part of the day. As you move to the reception hall after the ceremony, get it plugged in there. Place drained batteries in the charger; get that battery rotation organized through the day, so you always have a good battery supply.

Using Lights

There are two opinions about lighting among wedding videographers. Some of them use "unobtrusive lighting" as a selling point in their advertisement. It might as well be translated as "I can't afford the lighting kit" or "I don't care about lighting". The truth is: your camera won't be able to create an image without light. Therefore the light is your major tool along with your camcorder.

Speeches are the major part of the evening. If covering the speeches during the reception is part of your plan, take it seriously. Don't rely on available light. There might not be one. Your camera light may not be strong enough. And if you are planning to stand with your camera light right in front of the podium, you may block the person speaking from the rest of the audience. Not good.

Set up stationary lighting kit. Be in the room well in advance. If necessary, leave your previous location earlier. Find out where the speeches are going to be delivered from. In most cases it is going to be a podium. Find a location for your camera before the reception has started even if the speeches are not scheduled until the end of the dinner.

Grandparents of the Bride and the Groom

Never underestimate the significance of these quiet people often watching from aside as the wedding day progresses.

Find the grandparents at each location and follow them throughout the day. Get a glimpse at the bride's or groom's house, during the ceremony (a must!), posing for the group photo after the ceremony, some shots during the reception. Your attention will be much appreciated later on by the newlyweds.

Divorced Parents

You may sooner or later encounter a delicate problem of how to videotape divorced parents both present at the wedding. It is not as trivial as one may think.

There are few staged shots you may want to call, like asking parents to say few words on camera, or have parents blessing their daughter or son. Before you run into a problem, ask the bride, what is appropriate in the situation, and who does she want to see in the final video.

It may depend on many factors, like how long before the wedding the parents have been divorced, or if one or both side remarried, and probably most important - who is paying for the wedding.

In any case keep your coverage balanced, paying equal share of attention to all parents through the wedding day.

The End

This is the end of my guide. I hope you enjoyed reading it, and will do a great job covering the Big Day. Good luck!

At the very end you will find a checklist with

suggested key moments of the wedding day we have discussed in the book. Take it with you and check your coverage against the list to make sure nothing has been missed.

Wedding Day Checklist

Groom's House:
- the groom and his mother;
- guys having a drink;
- a few words from the groomsmen;
- best wishes from mom and dad;
- blessing;
- outdoor activity;
- house decoration.

Bride's House:
- a wedding dress;
- bride getting dressed;
- father meeting the bride;
- bride meeting a flower girl;
- blessing or parents wishes;
- bridesmaids wishes;
- formal photos;
- house decoration;
- bride leaving for the church.

Wedding Ceremony

- church exterior;
- arrival of the guests;
- arrival of the bride;
- bridesmaids walking down the aisle;
- the bride and her father walking down the aisle;
- the groom meeting the bride;
- candle shot (optional);
- readings (optional);
- exchange of vows;
- exchange of the rings;
- signing ceremony;
- communion;
- announcement of the marriage;
- married couple leaving the church;
- group photo on the front steps;
- guests greetings;
- bride and groom leaving the spot.

Wedding Reception

- cocktail hour;
- decoration of a banquet hall;
- receiving line;
- bridal party introduction;
- Prayer;
- toasts;
- speeches;
- gift table;
- formal dances;
- games;
- cake cutting;
- the guests dancing;
- bouquet toss;
- garter toss;
- sweet table.